Growing up at Uluṟu

AUSTRALIA

Story and pictures
by Stan Breeden

Right in the middle of Australia
stands a huge red rock.

The rock and the country around it belong to a group of
Aboriginal people called Pitjantjatjara and Yankunytjatjara.
These are very difficult words.
So, the people say, call us Anangu. It is easier.

Anangu call the big smooth rock Uluru.

Renita, Enid, Christopher
and Manu live at Uluṟu.

They like to play with their friends out on the wide plain. There they find fruits on the bushes and flowers full of nectar. These are good to eat.

The children's grandparents were born not far from Uluru. When the old people were young they could find all the food they needed in the bush.

There were no shops and supermarkets then. All the things they used like spears and dishes they made themselves.

The grown-up people still know how to live in the bush. Often they take the children out so that they too can learn about bush foods and other important things in Anangu life.

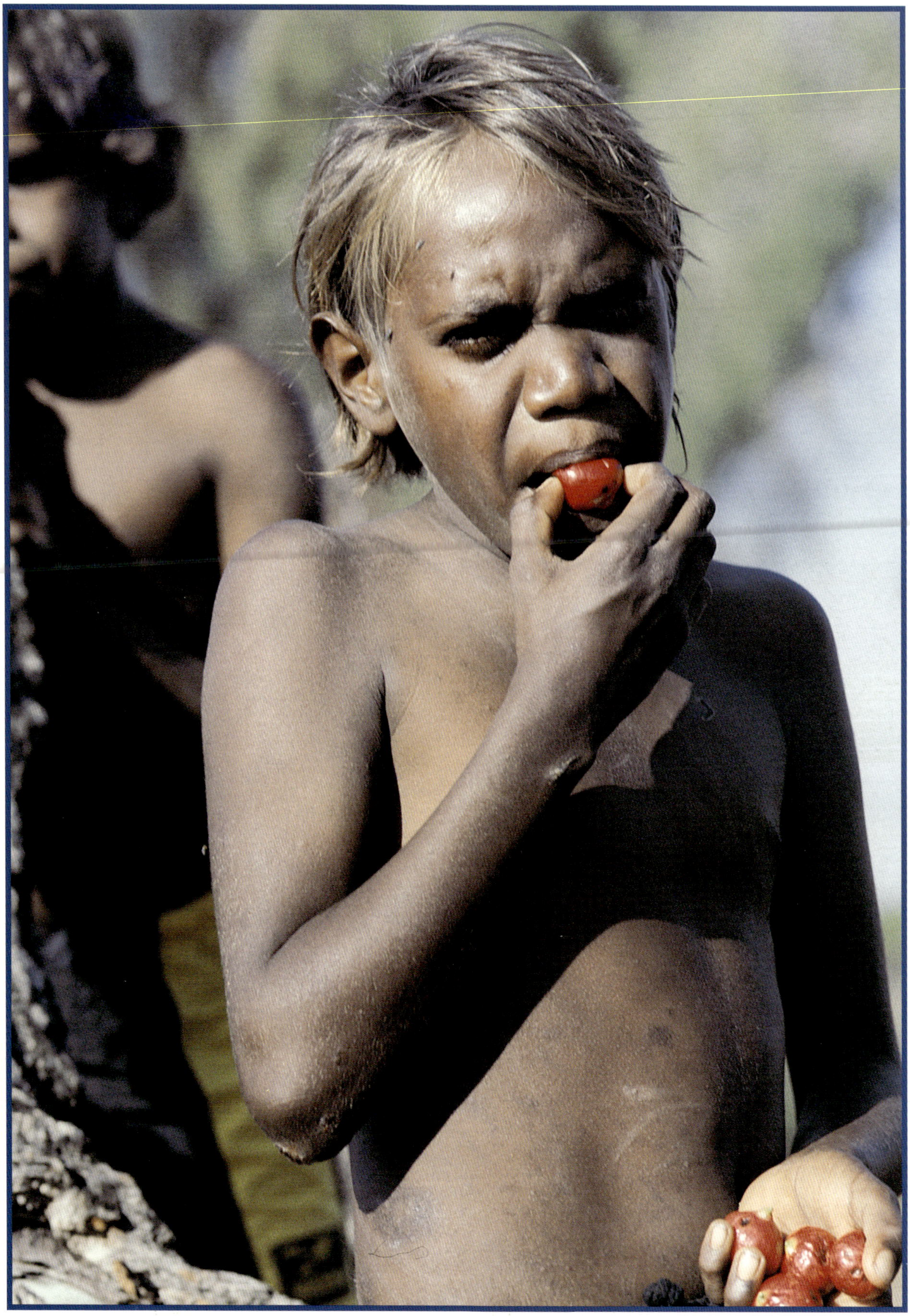

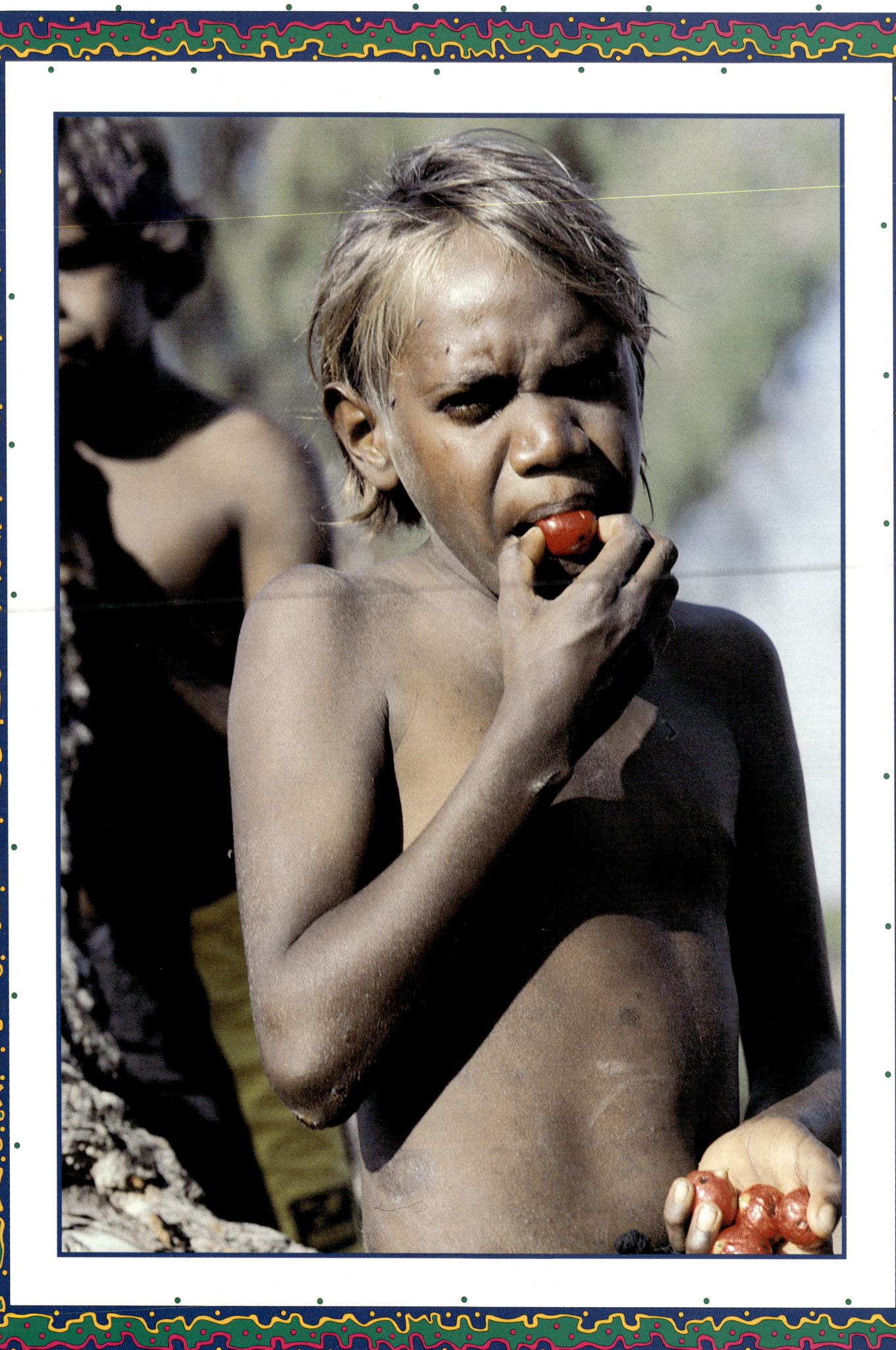

Out on trips to look for bush food, which they call bush tucker, they find many sweet fruits.

Daniel has found a Mangata or quandong tree full of bright red fruit.

Manu's mother Elizabeth and her friend Katy gather wild bush tomatoes. They call them Kampurarpa.

Christopher sucks the nectar from honey grevillea flowers - just as the birds do.

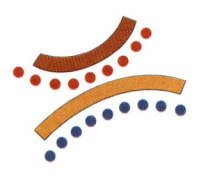

Barbara Tjikatu picks seed pods from a Wakalpuka bush, which is a kind of wattle. Back home she will grind them into flour to make bread.

Animals that live under the ground are also delicious to eat. Manu helps his mother to dig for Maku, or witchetty grubs. These live inside the roots of bushes.

Manu likes the soft velvet feel of the huge caterpillars. When cooked they taste sweet and nutty.

Maureen Natjuna loves the honey collected by ants. She digs deep down into the nest of Tjala ants.

Some of the ants are so swollen with honey they are like tiny pots.

Maureen gathers them up and puts them in a dish to take to her grandchildren.

While digging, Anangu often find lizards like Tinka the sand goanna. They too are good tucker.

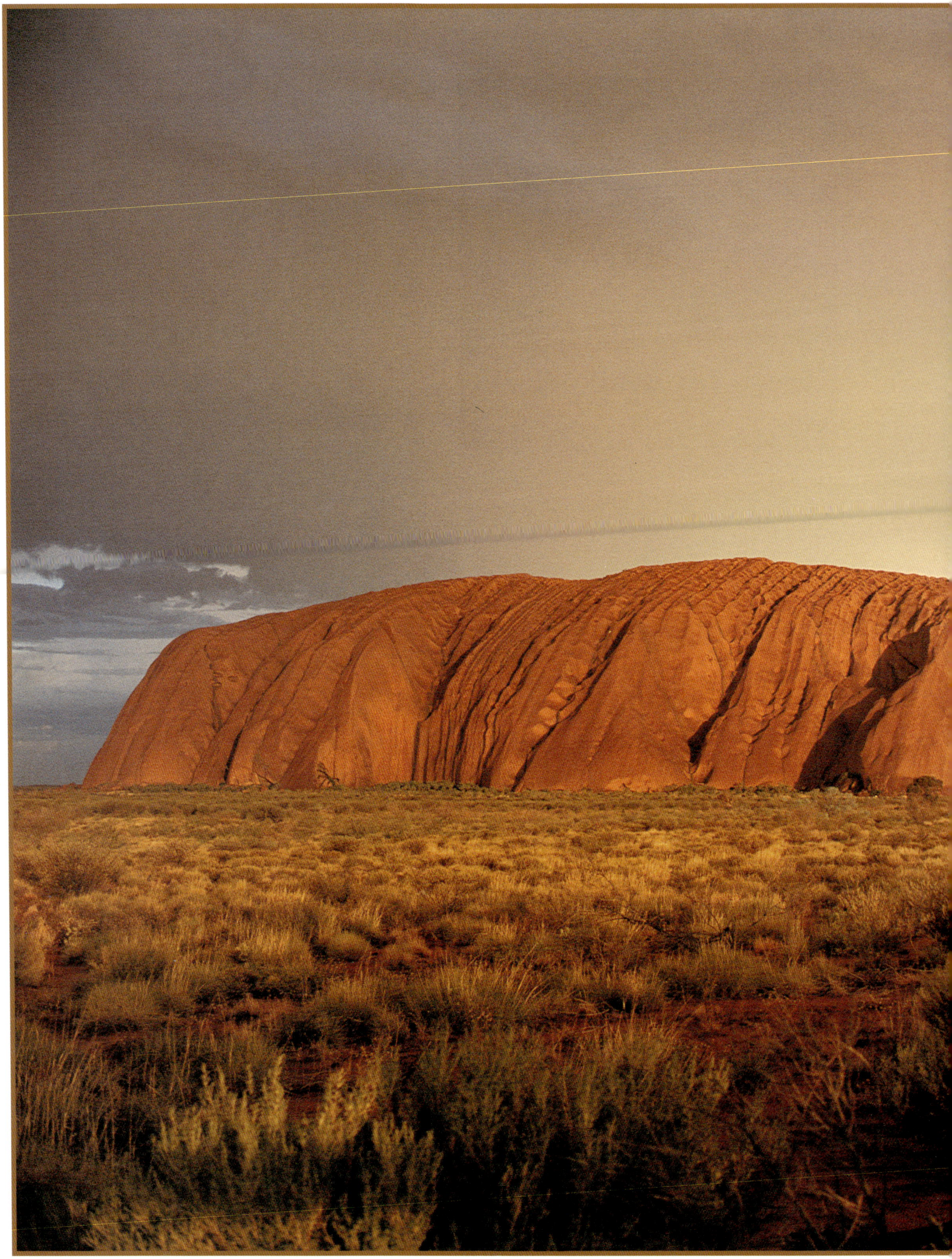

Whenever they go out into their country the children can see the huge rock of Uluru. It is very important to Anangu.

One of the elders, Tony Tjamiwa, tells the children stories about special places around Uluru and about the animals that made them.

Long, long ago, he tells them, in the time of the Tjukurpa, which non-Aborigines call the Dreamtime, the animals gave shape to some of the rocks.

At that time a young woma python, or Kuniya, was surprised by a group of Liru, which are venomous snakes. They threw spears at the python and killed him. So hard did they throw their spears that the points made holes in the rock.

The boy's aunt, also a Kuniya, was so angry that she killed one of the Liru with her stick.

These are the holes made in the rock by the points of the Lirus' spears. You can still see them today.

Kuniya the woma python can still be seen as a dark wavy line on Uluru.

Another story Tjamiwa tells is about how you must never be greedy and dishonest.

In the time of the Tjukurpa, he says, the Pan-pan-pal-al-a brothers, the crested bellbirds, went out hunting.

They found the tracks of Kalaya the emu and followed the tall bird. Moving slowly and quietly they came so close to Kalaya that they threw their spears. One spear went right through the emu, yet it did not die. It ran away, still carrying the spear. The brothers lost its tracks.

Lungkata the blue-tongued lizard was out hunting close to Uluru that same morning. He saw the wounded emu and killed it for himself. Immediately he cut it into pieces, built a fire and began to cook the meat. The emu really belonged to the Panpanpalala brothers and Lungkata knew it was wrong to steal it.

The bellbird brothers soon found Kalaya's tracks again and followed them to Lungkata's cooking fire. Frightened, Lungkata ran away, dropping pieces of meat all over the ground. He scrambled up Uluru to his camp in a cave high on the rock.

The brothers lit a fire beneath the cave. The smoke and heat made Lungkata dizzy. He slipped and fell to his death.

You can still see the pieces of emu meat Lungkata dropped. They turned to stone.

Here is an emu leg. It also turned to stone.

This pile of rocks at the base of Uluru is the remains of Lungkata's broken body.

Not far from Uluru are huge domes of rock standing closely together. Narrow valleys run between them. Anangu call these domes Kata Tjuta which means Many Heads. They are even higher than Uluru.

Kata Tjuta has secret and sacred places where only the men may go. It is a dangerous place for children.

They can only look at Kata Tjuṯa from a distance.

Sometimes they are allowed to peek into the narrow valley at Olga Gorge.

The soil around Uluru is red sand for as far as you can see.

The children love to play in the sand.

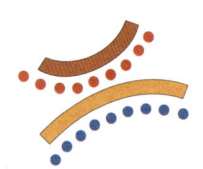

Daniel has drawn what he calls a Mamu, a horrible monster, that comes out at night and frightens Anangu children.

After heavy rain the sand is covered with wildflowers.

All the animals leave their footprints in the sand. Anangu, by looking at these tracks, can tell exactly which animals have made them, where they were going and what they were doing.

Edith Richards is an expert tracker. She shows the children the zigzag path left by a small poisonous snake and the tracks of a beetle.

Ngiyari the thorny devil leaves its footprints and casts a large shadow. A crested pigeon's footprints look as though they have been made by small sticks pressed into the sand.

Edith makes a perfect set of tracks of Papa the dingo with her fingers.

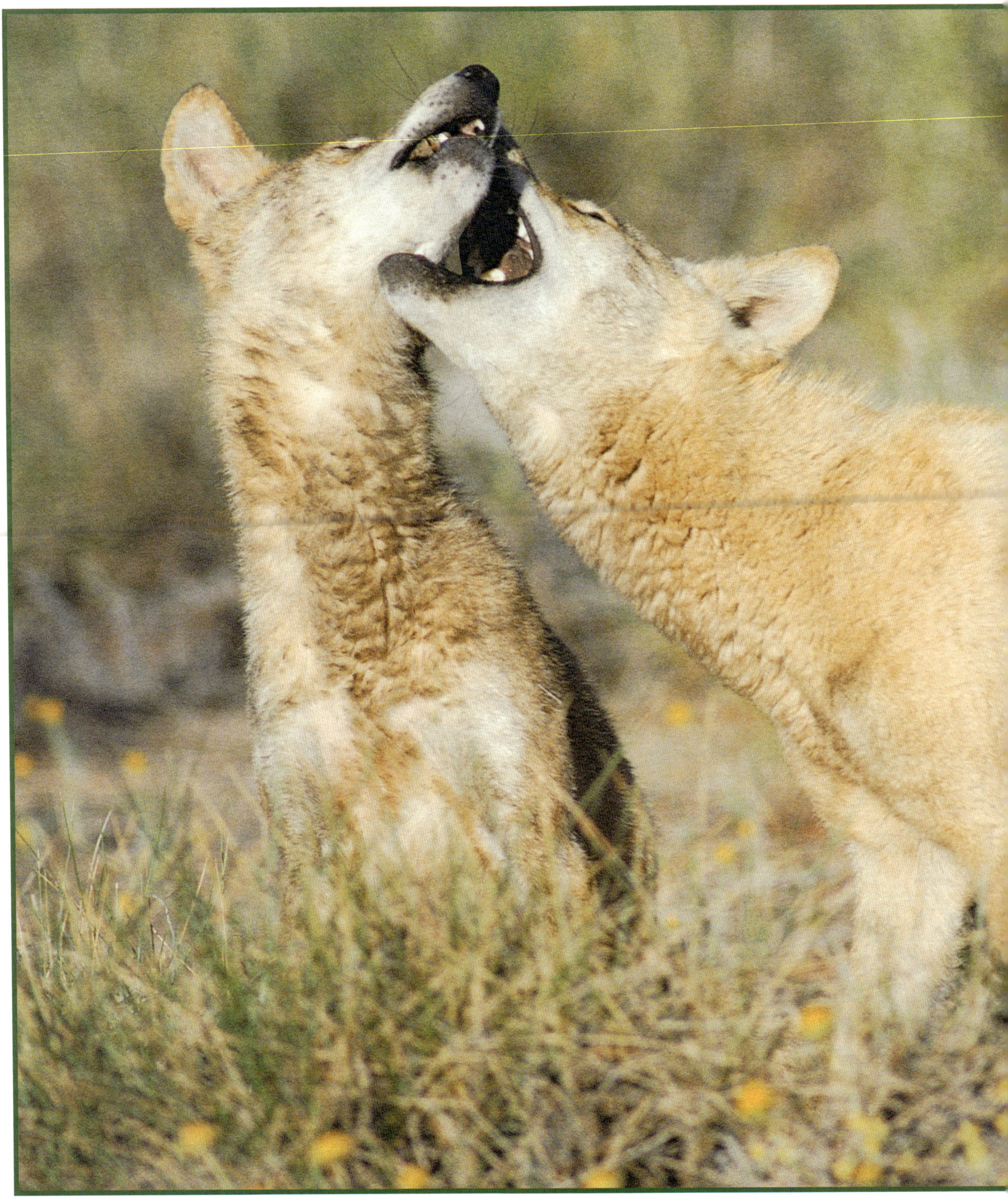

The children often see dingoes and their tracks.

Rhonda likes to go out bush with her father Ivan. He shows her special places and tells her about how the birds, lizards, insects and mammals live.

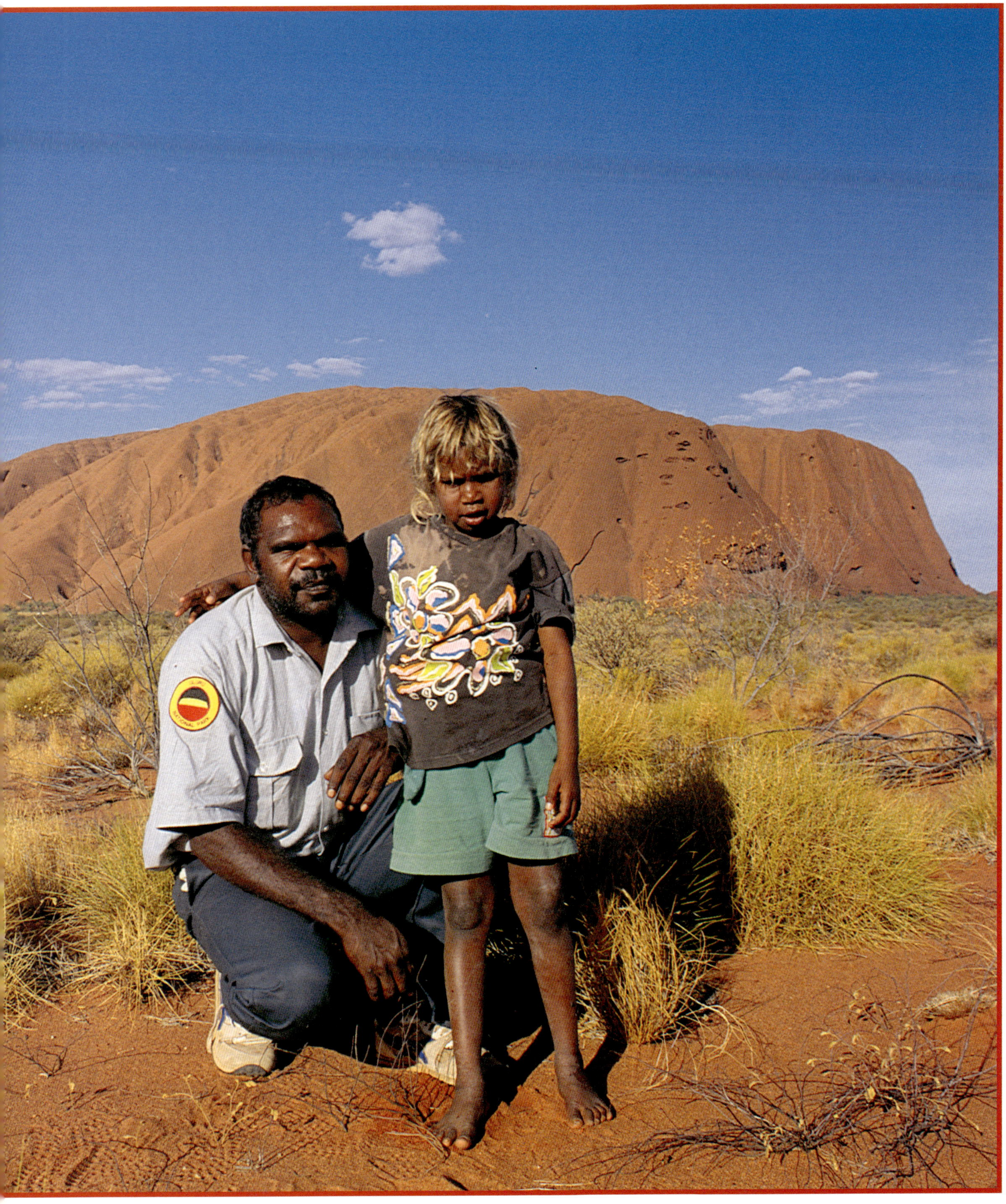

Usually so little rain falls at Uluru that it is almost a desert. But sometimes there is heavy rain that soaks deep into the sand.

During spring, after the rain, wildflowers of all colours spring up. Some are even green. Many insects come to their nectar.

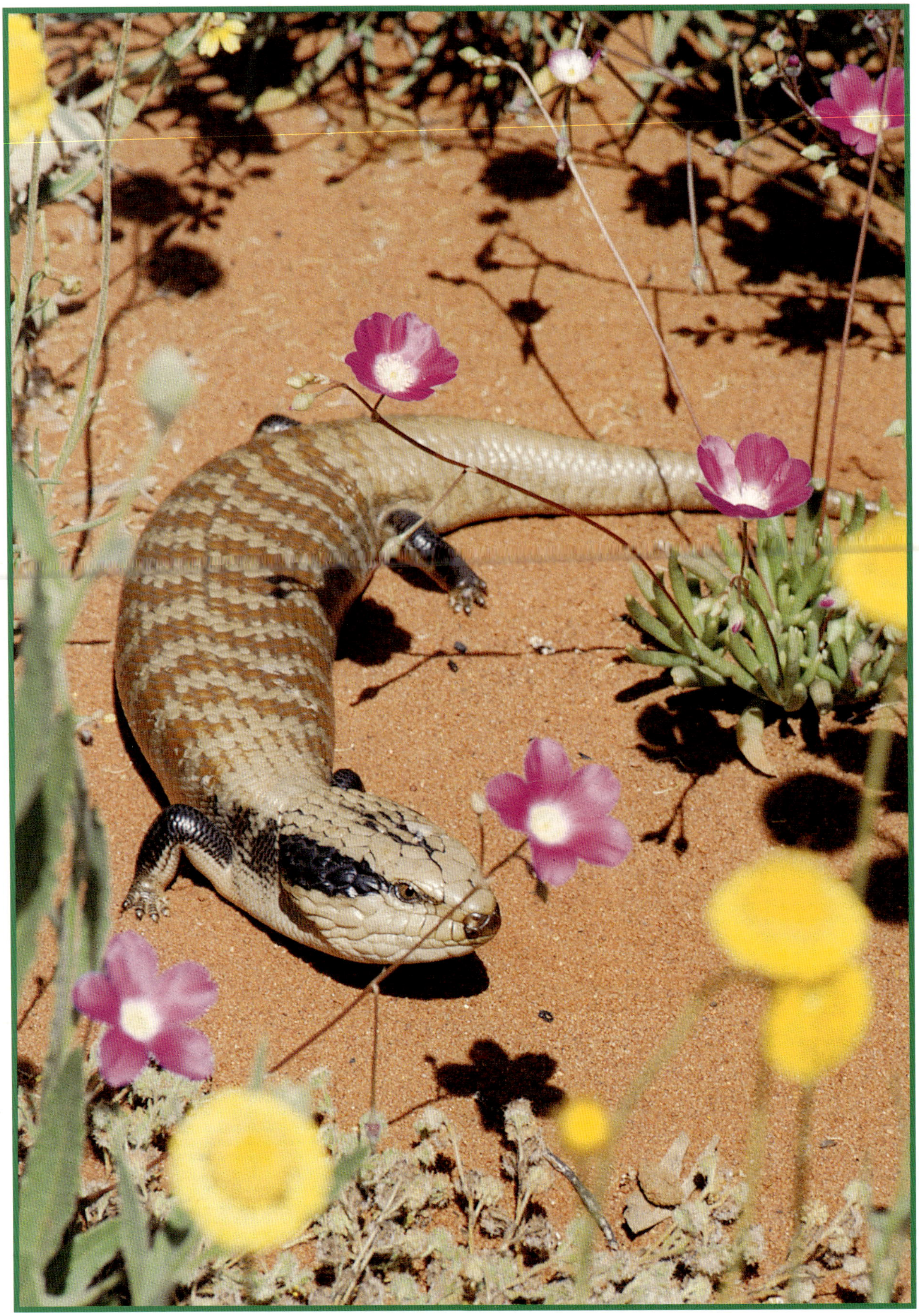

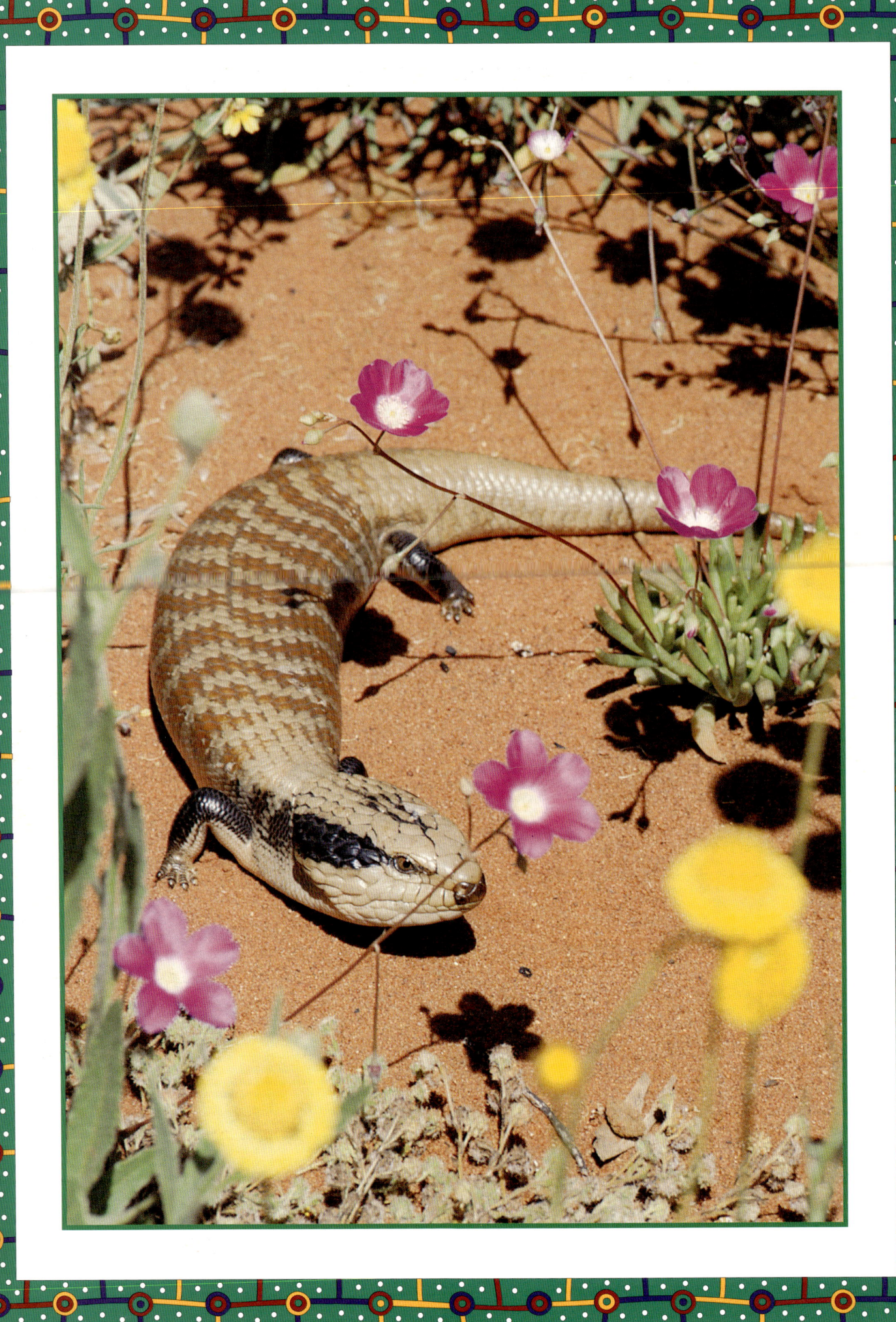

Bright sunshine on lizards, other animals, flowers, sand and rocks creates a world of dazzling colour. Uluru, after rain, is one of the most colourful places in the world.

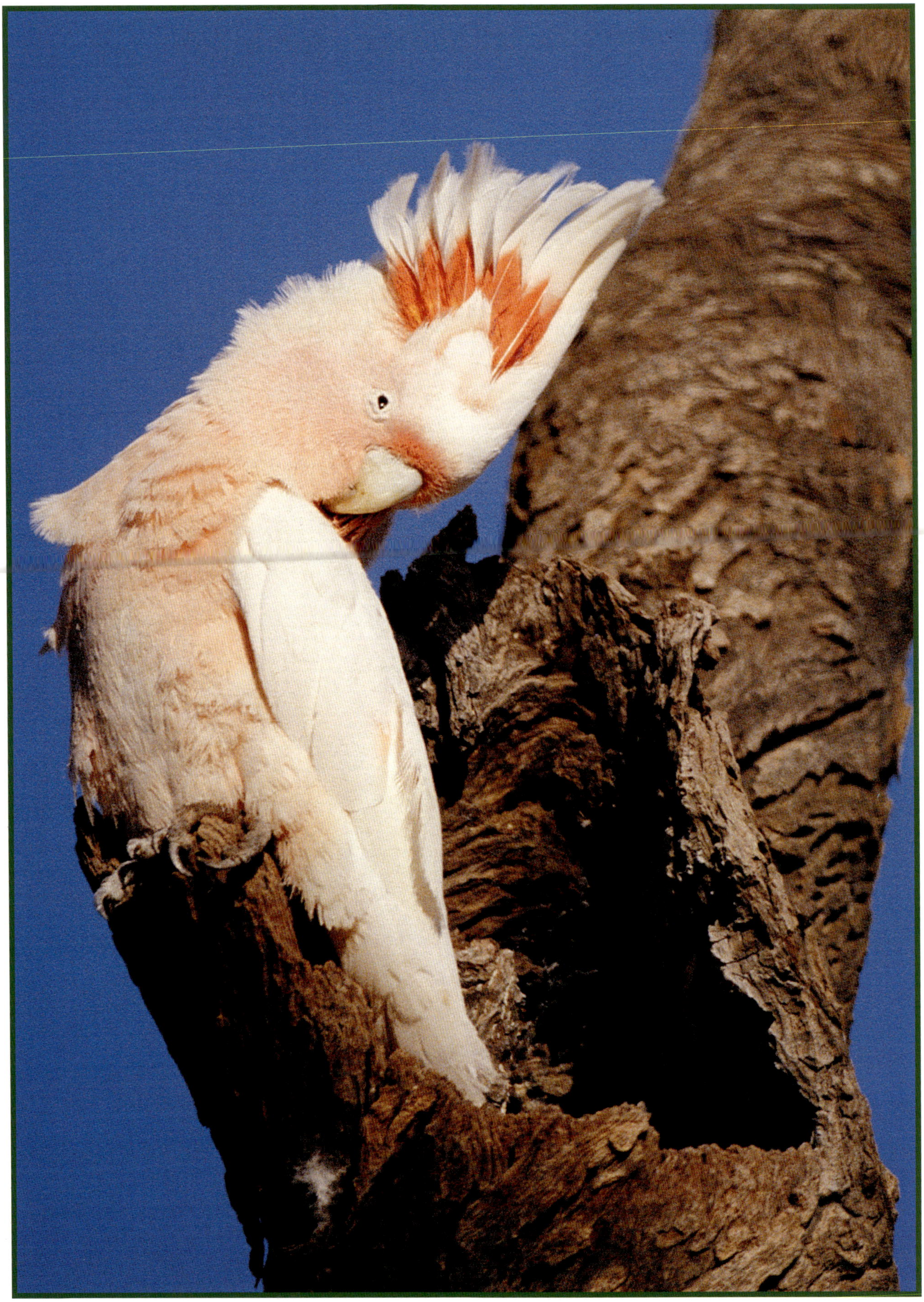

Birds come to feed on the insects, the flowers, and the seeds.

Lizards and small mammals also eat the insects.

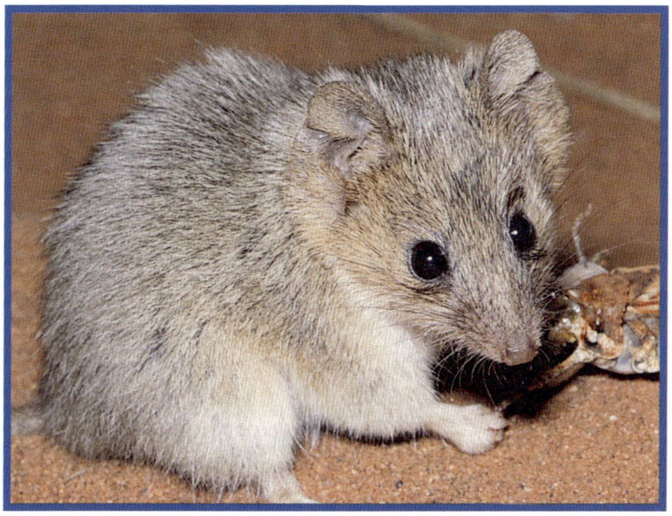
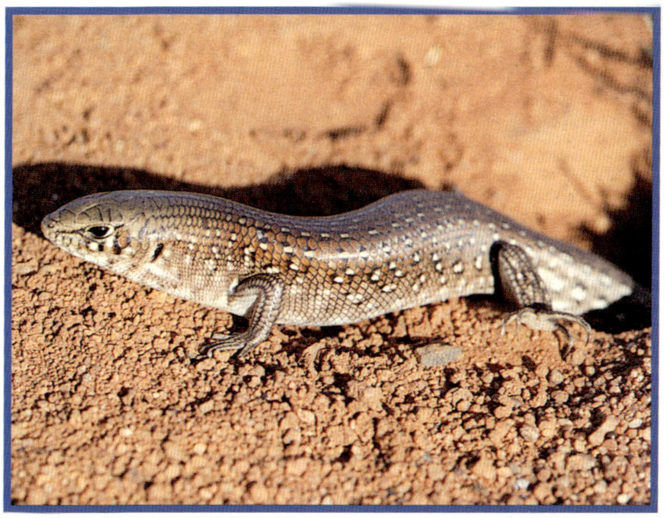
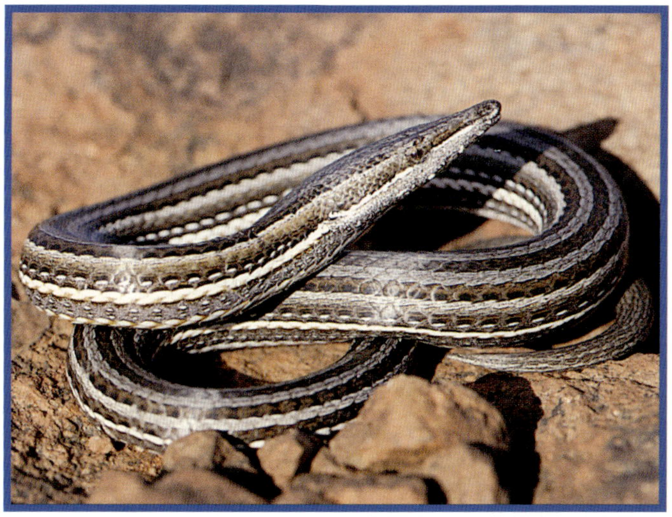
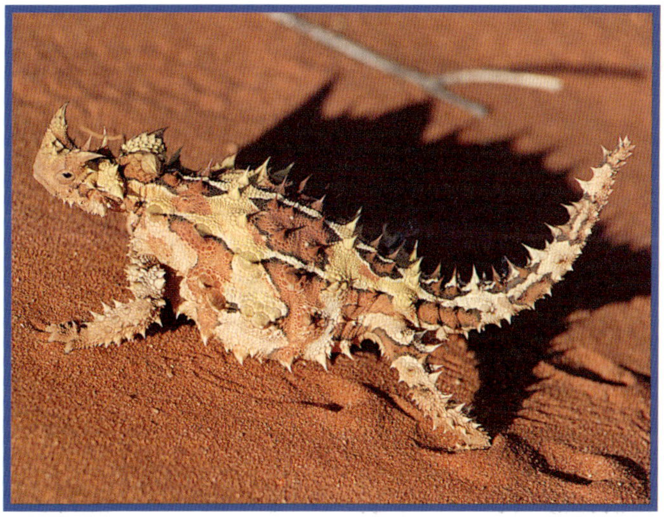
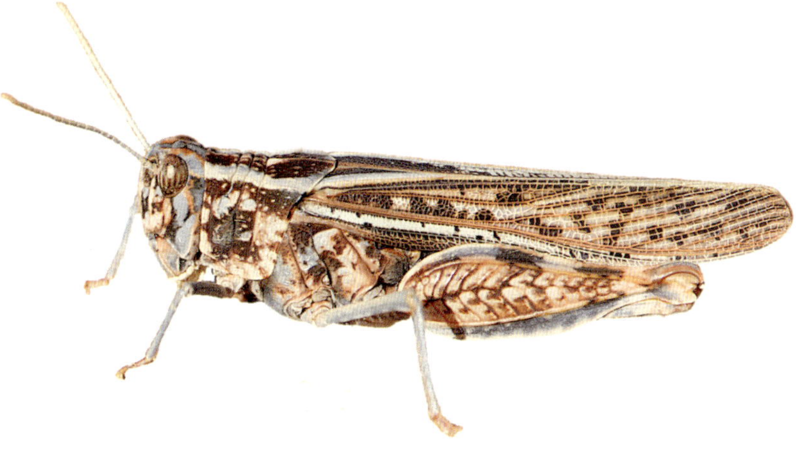

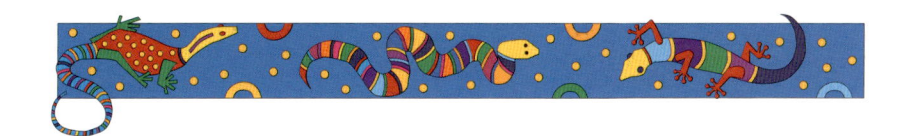

Norman Tjalkalyiri, an Anangu elder, walks through a very prickly grass called spinifex. When these grasses are very, very old they grow so closely together that other plants cannot live among them.

Anangu elders know just when the spinifex, which they call Tjanpi, has got too old. Then they burn it.

The fire hisses and crackles. When the wind is behind it, the fire roars along faster than the children can run. It is dangerous to get close. The children watch from far away.

After the fire, the country is bare and dry. It looks as if nothing will ever grow there again. But after rain there will soon be fields and fields of flowers.

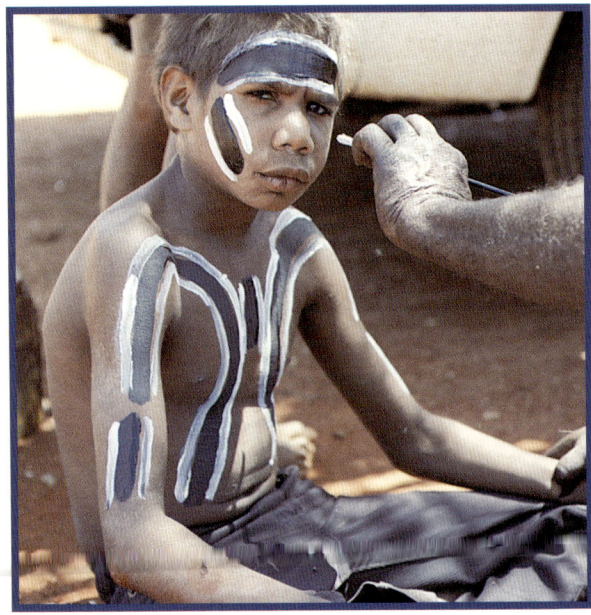

Back home the grown-ups tell the children Anangu stories in songs and dances.

The children are painted for these ceremonies.

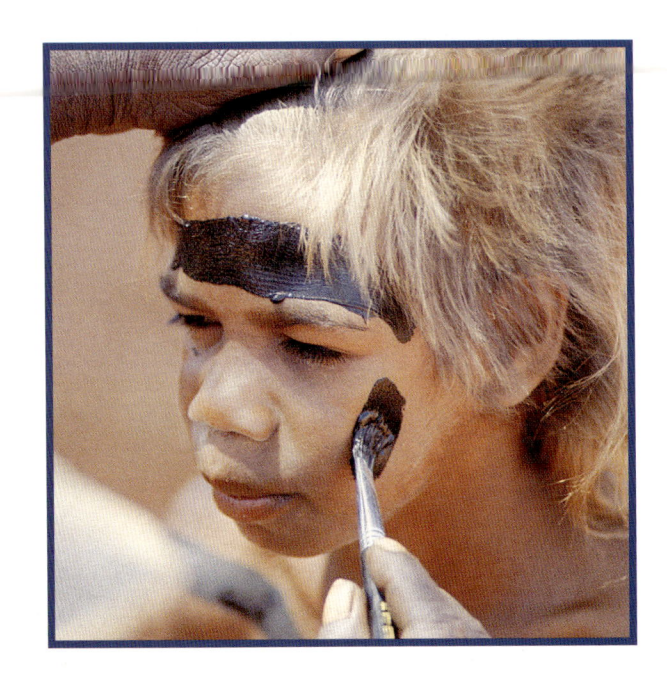

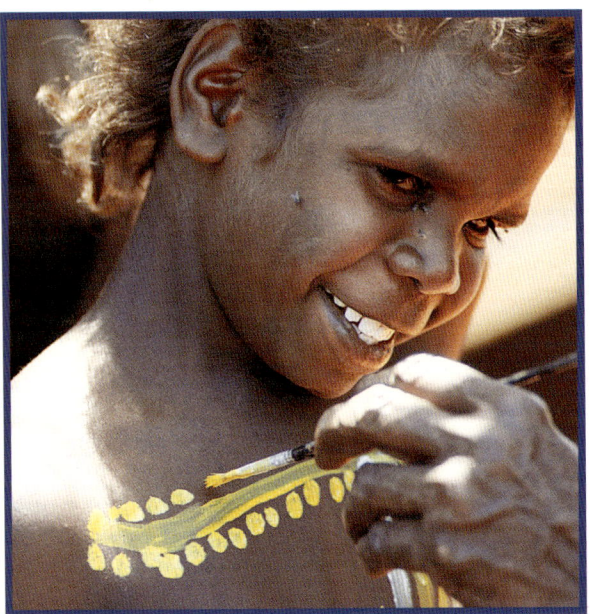

They learn about plants and animals, fire and bush tucker.

The girls sing and dance the story of Kuniya the python.

The boys act the story of Lungkata the blue-tongued lizard.

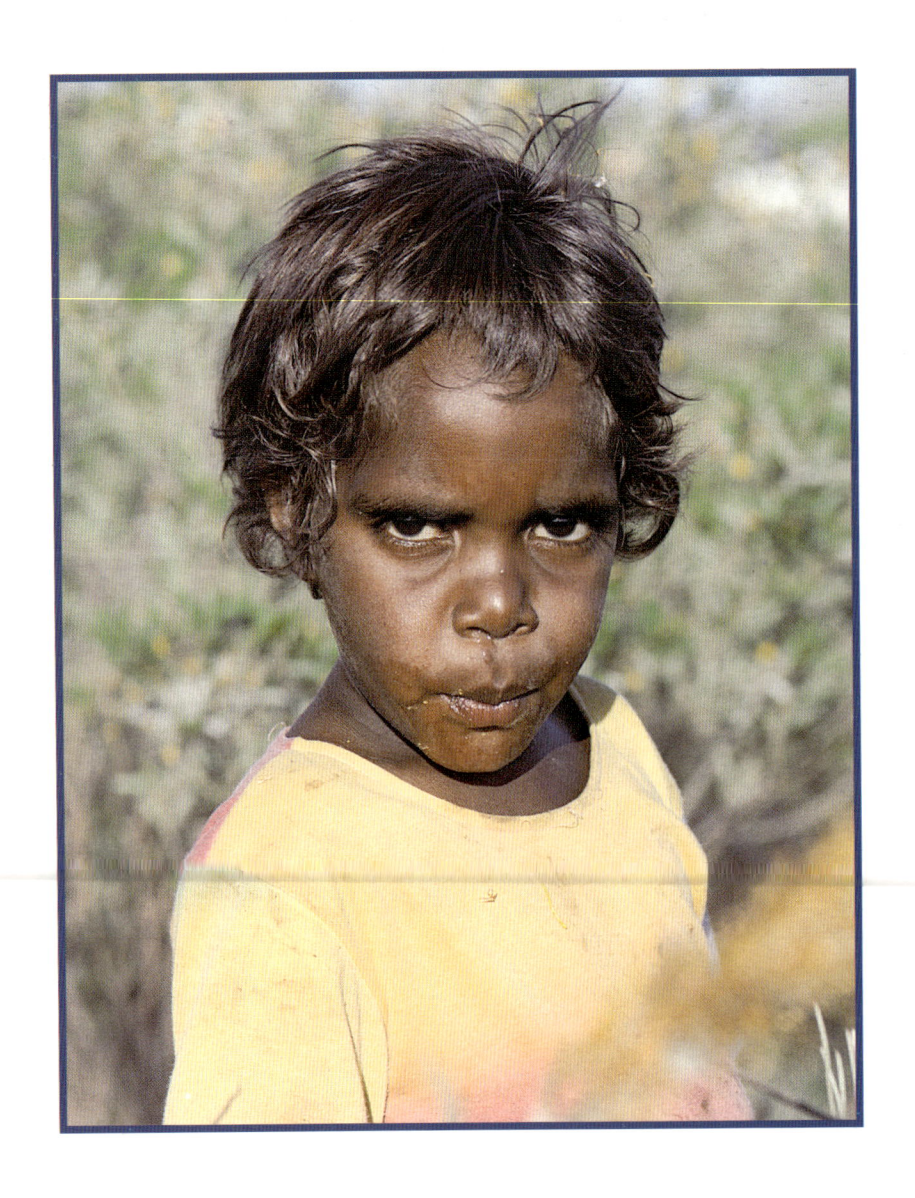

When the children grow up they will know how to look after Uluru and all their lands around the great red rock.